PLANNING, PREPARATION

& GUIDE

FOR THE FUTURE OF CHILDREN

By John Henry Jr.

Planning, Preparation & Guide For The Future Of Children

By Henry Jr., John 1947 to present

Copyright © 2016 by John Henry Jr.

Library of Congress Cataloging – in Publication Data

ISBN 978-0-692-90139-7

Registration Number TXu 2-0320600

Service Request Number 1-4208548181

November 28, 2016

All rights reserved. Printed in the United States Of America. No part of this publication may be reproduced or used in any way whatsoever without the express written permission of the author except for brief quotations in critical reviews or articles.

jhjre154640@gmail.com

Foreword

This is not just a book; it's a carefully crafted program that fosters many of the attributes and traits not taught in the current educational system. This tool adopts a low-tech approach to aid in echoing several key points, including the value of the dollar, the need for self-confidence, the significant impact of outside influences, and the imperative to plan, adjust, and adapt. Students of this course are reminded and encouraged to begin with an end in mind and working backward from their dreams, take positive and decisive steps toward turning them into reality.

This program is not designed to be completed once, but to be done periodically as the dreams and realities of the world we live in, shifts. Designed to point out the disparities in the student's current trajectory and desired one, this course should be used to help realign one's reality to reach their dream. In fact, this program will also serve as an excellent barometer to measure a participant's ability to weather the realities of life. I look forward to hearing about how my father's dreams positively impact your child's or student's reality.

Very Respectfully,
Zachary N. Henry
(Your Oldest Son)

Preface

Hello, my name is John Henry Jr. I am a Minister Of The Gospel Of The Lord Jesus Christ. I have been married for forty-five years and my wife and I have six children; four girls and two boys.

One day, in an effort to help our oldest child become better prepared for her future, I was inspired by God to sit down at the kitchen table with her to find out what were her interests, goals in life and her plans for the future. At this time, computers were not available for public use, so we looked through the News Paper for the information we needed and wrote down her ideas and thoughts.

When she concluded her life's choices, it did not look so good to me, considering the harshness of the era of the times that we were living in. Nevertheless, God blessed her. She went on to graduate Cum Laude from Aurora University with a Bachelor Of Liberal Studies in Secondary Education. She was employed as an English Teacher and Dean of Students at a Local High School, here in Chicago.

It must be noted that often times, as parents, we make decisions for our children, while they are young and still growing up. For instance, we decide what they are going to wear, what school they would go to, whether they play sports or not, etc. It should also be noted that some people make decisions emotionally, out of envy, or with the desire to keep up with The Joneses. Rarely is a decision made out of a personal, heartfelt desire or choice. Outside influences often affect people and cause them to make decisions that they soon regret.

The purpose of this book is to inspire parents to help their children realize the facts of life that they will soon face. It is your job to show them what it is going to take for them to be ready for the realities of adulthood. With all of the new technologies that are evolving, they will need to know how to make it through the rough times and live with less and nothing.

As a parent, it is your job to prepare your children for the unforeseen weight of responsibilities that is hidden from their eyes. They need to know how to take care of themselves when they are on their own. This book gives them a sample of true life issues and helps them to choose what steps it is going to take, to enjoy it one day.

Parents, you can only help them so far. It is up to them to make it when you are not holding their hands. Therefore, use this book as a Handbook to guide them to choose wisely. The choices they make will be what they will have to live with for the rest of their lives.

This book is like a Handbook that will guide you as a parent to show your child some of the facts of life. Everybody is different and that includes our children. Many children follow in their parent's footsteps and do whatever their parents do or did. Even though they are not our size; cannot wear our clothes or see through our glasses, etc., we have to allow them the freedom to make their own mistakes and love them anyway.

As hard as it may be and as disappointed as we may become, we must only guide them objectively with the Pros and Cons of their choices while they select them. In other words, we must allow them to make these decisions no matter how we feel about them. Eventually, if they see that they made the wrong choices, they have time to turn around and start all over again. That is why we recommend that you hold on to this book, because you may need to sit down with your child and revisit some of his/her decisions and try something else. You may also use it with your other children.

When my oldest son graduated from the Naval Academy, he changed out of the Navy Uniform that he was wearing into a Marine Corp. Uniform. This was heartbreaking for me because, before he entered college, he said to me that he wanted to follow in my footsteps and go into the Navy. When my wife and I found that out, we pulled out all stops to get him into the Naval Academy. Additionally, there was a war going on in Iraq and Afghanistan that I feared he would not make it through as a Marine with boots on the ground. Nevertheless, I had to step back and allow him to make his own decision. This was his life and at that time, being a Marine was how he wanted to spend it. As hard as it was for his mother and me, we prayed for his safe return and God blessed. He made it back without a scratch. **HALLELUJAH!**

As our family grew, this same intervention was helpful in guiding all of our children to find the path that helped them be successful. As a result, some of them have graduated from College with honors, joined the military, and became a nurse and a teacher. I am confident this same method of preparation can be helpful and beneficial to all parents, teachers, and their children/students, which is why I was inspired to write this book.

The programs in this book are designed to help children become better prepared for many of life's changes. They show children, step by step how to figure out what they want to be for the rest of their lives. They also will show them how to budget for their future while choosing important items for a good Cost Estimate of the choices they make. They will even help them decide if they want to go to

College or just get married.

Parents, depending on that child's maturity, it will be helpful to define the Advantage, Benefit, Strength and/or Quality of the subjects of each section of this book. I leave that up to you because you know your child/student better than I do. However, by defining the topics of each section, you will help your child/student to see the value of that topic in that section and by them, now knowing the definition of that topic, they will be influenced to make a wise choice. Additionally, you might want to research deeper into a particular subject to learn more information about it to help guide them in their decisions and choices.

Introduction

Within this book, you will help your child make choices about Housing, Furniture, Clothing and the type of Food/Groceries they may want to buy. Additionally, you can guide them to select the type of Vehicle/Car or SUV/Truck they want to drive. You will also lead them as they look at what type of Insurance (Protection, Coverage) they will need to carry for their Health, Life, Dentist, Eye Care, Vehicle, apartment or Home.

At the end of each Subject is a Table to be filled out of their own selections. These Tables are designed to write down/record your child's decision of the lifestyle they want to lead. Once your child has finished filling out each Subject Table of the life they want to live, help them total up all of the finances of each table. Therefore, help them to look closely at what Career will be best for them to maintain the lifestyle they want. Consider this, they will also need a good Banking system to be able to pay for their products and services.

Finally, write the totals of each Table on the **Total Cost of Living Estimate Table**. With this total, they will have a general view of what type of Income it is going to take to achieve and sustain the lifestyle they want.

At the same time, once they finish, you will be proud you showed them how to, step by step, figure out many of life's challenges. They are a few steps closer to their bright future and what they will have to do to achieve the goals that they have set.

At this time, go over these questions with them and help them get a better glimpse of their future:

- What High School and College do I want to go to?
- For that High School and College I want to attend, am I studying hard enough in school to get the required GPA?
- What Career do I want?
- Am I working hard enough now, in school, to get the career that I want and have a successful lifestyle that I have planned for?
- If not, then what must I do now, to achieve my goals?

In asking these questions, they will have to think about how planning now can help them reach their goals. They should not be concerned about what's going on around them or what their friends think and say about them and their decisions? Ask them, can their friends live your life for you? Will they come to your rescue and bail you out when you need them?

Show them **THAT IT IS ALL LEFT UP TO THEM!** No one can be the judge of what they decide to do with their life. Consequently, since this is their life, they have to decide what they want for themselves. Tell them, **THIS IS YOUR LIFE AND ONLY YOU ARE RESPONSIBLE FOR HOW IT TURNS OUT.** If you do not prepare for it, it will not be your friend's fault, it will be yours. You cannot allow friendship or the impact of your friends to affect your decisions. It is your decision to make and it all depends on you and how you feel about yourself and your surroundings. Get them to stop and ask themselves these questions:

- Do you like where you live or do you want something better?
- Do you like how you look or do you want to wear better-looking clothes?
- Are you happy making the type of grades you are making?

Make it clear to them, **IT IS ALL LEFT UP TO YOU! THIS IS YOUR LIFE AND**

YOU CAN MAKE IT BETTER OR NOT!

As you continue through this program with them, get them to look in the mirror of their life and see where they stand. The cost of living is higher than it was when they were a small child. With that thought in mind, have they prepared for getting older? Are they ready to become an adult?

Times are changing with greater and more advanced technology. Ask them, are you prepared to meet or deal with the changes in this world? Help them to see that now is the time for them to start to look at their future as they grow and gain strength. Get them to **STOP AND TAKE TIMEOUT TO PLAN FOR THEIR FUTURE!** Decide now, **WHAT DO YOU WANT TO BE WHEN YOU GROW UP?**

Acknowledgment

In view of the loss of my oldest daughter, and the fact that she was the first child to go through this program, I dedicate this book to her memory: Wenona C. Williams (maiden name Henry). Thank you for being your father's first Guinea Pig. Your memory will always be with your mother and me.

I also dedicate this book to the rest of my children who have also gone through this program. I hope it helped you to succeed in life.

Peace be unto you all,

Father

TABLE OF CONTENTS
THE PROGRAM

PLANNING THE FUTURE

A Good Starting Time	13-14
Important Items Needed	15
Ambition & Career Goal Section & Table	16-23
Marriage Section & Table	24-26

EDUCATION

The High School Section & Table	27-29
The College Section & Table	30-33

BUDGETING & EXPENSES

City Where Would You Like To Live Section & Table	34-36
The Type of Housing You Planning to Have Section & Table	37-38
The Type of Automobile You Want Section & Table	39-41
Your Grocery Bill Section & Table	42-45
Your Clothing Allowance Section & Table	46-48
Furniture Section & Table	49-51
Insurance Section & Table	52-54
Banking Section & Table	55-57

TOTAL LIVING EXPENSES

Total Living Expenses Table	58
Total Income Needed To Sustain This Lifestyle Table	59
Sex, Alcohol, and Drugs	60-61
Final Words & Decision Making	65-64
References	65

THE PROGRAM
PLANNING FOR THE FUTURE

A Good Starting Time

To The Parent:

The best time to start this program is when one is in their early teens. It's easier at this age because you can keep moving forward. It is not impossible, but it gets harder as you get older. Plus, the sooner you start this, the sooner you can progress. Life is tough. That is exactly why you should start now to achieve your goals. Starting now can give you an advantage for success and make you stronger.

I started this program with my children when they were beginning eighth grade, just before they entered high school. This is a time when they were looking at their future and had a lot of decisions to make.

To The Child/Student:

This program will guide you in the right direction to make the proper choices for your future. As a result of doing well in school, you can get your dream job and make lots of money. Why do this planning now? Because the earlier you start the closer you be to the future you want.

True, there is always something else you can do. Hanging out with your friends might be more fun than spending time planning for your future, but if you open your mind, this can be fun too and widen your horizons to life. You can have a good time and this Handbook will help you with your planning.

Your Parents will set aside some time for you when you get started. Therefore, bring paper, pencils or pens and the Classified Section of your newspaper. You may also have to use your computer to go on the Internet for more research material.

Your Parents will only assist you. **YOU MUST DO ALL OF THE WRITING AND RESEARCH TO ANSWER THE QUESTIONS AND FILL IN THE BLANKS YOURSELF**. Listen as your Parents go through this program with you step by step and discuss each item line by line. There are pros and cons of all of them. This Handbook will show you what it takes to make ends meet and what you must do now to accomplish your future goals. Once you have assembled this information, they will assist you and discuss with you your plans for the future. For instance:

- What Are Your Ambitions And Career Goals?
- What High School Would You Like To Attend?
- What College Would You Like To Go To?
- Where Would You Like To Live?
- What Type Of Housing Do You Plan To Have?
- What Automobile Do You Want To Drive?
- Do You Plan To Get Married?
- What Will Your Cost Of Living Expenses Be?
- How Much Money Do You Think You Need To Make Annually?

Important Items Needed

Here are some important items you need to gather:

- The Sunday Newspaper

    - The Advertising Section

    - The Classified Section showing Housing and Cars

    - The Business sections

- Magazine Ads, the Classified Section or Articles of your choice

- The Computer

    - From the Internet Find a List of Current Salaries By Occupation (to get a view of present-day Occupational Salaries)

Ambition & Career Goals

To The Parent:

What is an Ambition? What is a Career? Define these things for your child/student. Here are some definitions from Merriam-Webster. An Ambition is defined as to have a particular goal or aim or something that a person hopes to do or achieve, it reflects a desire to be successful, powerful, famous or to do things and be active. (https://www.merriam-webster.com/dictionary/ambition)

A Career is a profession for which one trains and which is undertaken as a permanent calling; your vocation, occupation, business, profession or job you indulge in, to support yourself and/or your family is your career. Your Career will depend on your ambitions and goals in life.

Be honest when defining the term Ambition and share what your Ambition (s) in life is/were. Talk about what you wanted to be while growing up. Show your child/student how far you got; where you went wrong; what you could have done to change your ways to get on the right track. This is important because it will show your child/student that you made some mistakes and you do not want them to follow in your footsteps. This moment of open truthfulness about your pass will help your child/student see what was right and wrong, depending on your outcome. This will also administer a bond and closeness between you and that child/student that they never had before.

Consequently, when planning for the future, your child's/student's Ambition/Career is the main thing to be concerned about. At this time, the desire and goals they will have set for themselves in life should be your ultimate purpose and focus.

To The Child:

You have a variety of Careers in many industries to choose from. For example, there is Agriculture, Aviation, Construction, Architecture, Materials Science, Electronics, Energy, Entertainment, IT and Communications, Medical, Neuroscience, Military, Outer Space, Robotics, and Transportation, just to name a few. Now, give it some thought and decide, **What Is Your Ambition Or Career Goal You Want To Set For Your Life?** With all of the advanced technology in this world, **What Type Of Career Are You Looking For?**

This is not a Buddy-Buddy Plan that you make; meaning your decision for your life is based on what your Buddy/Friend think or want you to do or do with them together. You are still young and your Buddy might change his mind or you move to another city or other tragic things may happen and change his or her future.

Therefore, this is a decision that you must make for yourself. Even though things are going to change your life, you must start somewhere and put forth some type of effort to determine what type of future you want for yourself. Do not be afraid, but look at all of the options and give it a try. If you do not like your first decision, you can always change your mind and try something else. So, ***What Do You Want To Be When You Grow Up***?

As you consider your life's Ambition or Career, here are some items you might what to look into, as you do your research. Does my desire Amibition/Career have Benefits, a good Salary, is in a good Location and are there any Prerequisites?

Benefits

Here is a Tip! Of all of the jobs available in the world, make sure you find a job that has benefits that will help you and your family. I find these benefits to be most important:

- Life Insurance - Family Plan
- Health Insurance - Family Plan
- Dental Insurance - Family Plan
- Eye Care Insurance for glasses - Family Plan
- Plan For Retirement, such as a 401K plan
- Stock Options

Having these benefits will assure you and your family safety and security throughout your career.

Here is another Tip! Do not be overly concerned about making a large Salary! I say that because when you look at the cost of the benefits and combine it with the Salary, together they will exceed the cash you will receive, and you do not have to pay out of your pocket for them. The Job pays for them for you.

Salary

Salaries are going to be dependent on the type of Job you find. Not all jobs pay high salaries because they cannot afford to. They have to pay what they can afford and make a profit to stay in business and provide a service to its customers. Therefore, they pay the Minimum Wages. Companies that pay more than that are, generally, paying it to employees that have been on the job and gone up the Salary PayScale. But all start at the bottom at or below Minimum Wages.

Consequently, do not expect to earn a large salary unless they bargain it with you when you are hired. Additionally, large salaries are given to people with a valuable Skill Set to offer a company. These skills often come because of a person's High Education and or Vocation Ability. In other words, the higher the education, the higher the pay, the lower the education, the lower the pay.

Below are a few options for different types of Careers. Select & record the one you like in the Table.

- **Over 12,000 Careers** - http://www.careerplanner.com/ListOfCareers.cfm
- **Salaries & Jobs** - http://www.salarylist.com/jobs/Other-Salary.htm
- **100 of the Best Jobs** - http://money.usnews.com/careers/best-jobs/rankings/the-100-best-jobs

Location

Job location depends on what city you live in or would like to live in and its availability in that city, state or country. While there are many different types of jobs in the world, they are not all located in the same area. Some are seasonal types of jobs that are located in climates to suit that seasonal job. Warm Vacation spots have jobs in them that are not located in the North or South Pole region.

Therefore, you might have to move to the area where your job is located and live there until you decide to move or do something else. Nevertheless, your Ambition will lead you to the location of the Career you seek. Consider this as you decide your Career:

- Is the location of the Career of my Ambition on a mountain or in a valley or on the level plain area?
- What type of climate is in the area of that type of job? (Tornados, Hurricanes, Earthquakes, etc.)
- Am I willing to make the sacrifice to move to that location?

Prerequisites

Prerequisite means something that you officially must have or do before you can have or do something else. They are basic, fundamental, essential required skills, abilities, talents or information you have from your experience or education. That is why it is important that now, while you are still in school, that you study hard and obtain all of the knowledge to perfect your abilities as you prepare for the rest of your life.

You may not see the connection, but what you do now in school will affect the rest of your life. If you neglect to study your assignments or do homework, it can affect you when you fill out a simple Job Application. As you study in school, you are building your Skill Set for the workplace on the Job you seek, in the Ambition you desire. Spelling, Math, Science, History, etc., are valuable prerequisites that will determine your ability to be hired and the salary you desire with the company you apply with.

Now, for the Ambition and Career goals you've set, investigate to see what prerequisites are required. Then examine yourself to see if you have those prerequisites or not to move forward toward them. Can you vision yourself with all of the cars you are going to drive or the type of house or apartment you are going to live in? What is it going to take for you to reach your goals? What do you need for the rest of your life? According to Dictionary.com, **Faith is the pre-requisite of every successful accomplishment in life.**

Take a few moments and jot down on the lines below, what you think your ambition might be and what you want for a career. Remember, you can always change your mind and start over.

_____
_____
_____
_____
_____
_____
_____
_____
_____
_____
_____
_____
_____
_____
_____
_____

The Ambition & Career Goals Table

Here is **The Table of Ambition, Benefits, And Career Goals**. After you have done your research Online, in the News Paper & Magazines, record your selection on the Table. Fill in the category of the Occupations, Locations, Prerequisites, Benefits, and Salaries from your selection. Fill in as many spots on the table you like, if you have more than one Ambition or Career Goal in your plans.

Below are a few options for different types of Careers.

- **Over 12, 000 Careers** - http://www.careerplanner.com/ListOfCareers.cfm
- **Salaries & Jobs** - http://www.salarylist.com/jobs/Other-Salary.htm
- **100 of the Best Jobs** - http://money.usnews.com/careers/best-jobs/rankings/the-100-best-jobs

OCCUPATION	LOCATION	PREREQUISITES	BENEFITS	SALARY

The Business Trip

Marriage

Marriage, according to Merriam-Webster Online Dictionary, is defined as the institution or a significant practice, relationship, or organization in a society or culture, whereby individuals are joined in a marriage; the state of being united in a legal relationship as husband and wife. It is also the state of being united to a person as a spouse in a legal, consensual, and contractual relationship recognized and sanctioned by and dissolvable only by law. Wikipedia, The Online Free Encyclopedia, defines marriage as matrimony or wedlock, is a socially or ritually recognized union between **spouses** that establishes rights and obligations between those spouses, as well as between them and any resulting biological or adopted children and **affinity** (in-laws and other family members through marriage).

Marriage is a very personal and sacred event to have in one's life because it starts a person's family. It is the first institution known to man. It is a very important step in one's life and needs serious thought. You have to be in love with another person to the degree that you are willing to sacrifice your future plans for that person. With that thought in mind, the two of you may need counseling for direction and guidance from a Minister to help you confidently decide how to carry yourselves until that wedding day.

There are a lot of things that go along with Marriage. Weddings have to be planned. Here are a few things to look at:

- What Day To Plan The Wedding
- Wedding Invitations
- Minister or Judge
- Wedding Location
- Size: How Large Shall Your Wedding Be
- Reception
- Dresses, Tuxedos, Wedding Party, Flowers, etc.
- Honey Moon Location
- Home or an Apartment
- Will you have children?
- Total Cost Of The Wedding

You and your Fiancé have to plan together, the type of wedding you want to have. After the Wedding, Reception and Honey Moon, where are you going to live? Your desires must agree with your spouse's desires. Remember, you are not alone anymore. Now it is, what's best for us. What shall we do today/tonight? Will my companion like this? Etc., Etc., Etc.

The Marriage Table

Here is **The Marriage Table**. After you have done your research Online, in the News Paper & Magazines, record your selection on the Table. Fill in the categories of the Wedding Day, Invitations, Location, Reception, Flowers, Dresses, Tuxedos, Honey Moon Locations, Etc., Etc., Etc.

(See Wedding Magazines or the Newspaper for Wedding Planning ideas.)

Marriage	When	Location	Size Of Wedding	Cost
Wedding Day				
Wedding Invitations				
Wedding Location				
Reception				
Flowers				
Dresses				
Tuxedos				
Wedding Party Size				
By Minister Or Judge				
Honey Moon Location				
Home Or Apartment				
Will We Have Children?				
Miscellaneous				
Total Cost				

EDUCATION

High School

The value of a High School Education is more important than you can imagine. The college you decide to attend will open or close its doors to you depending on your High School GPA. The jobs you apply for are going to look at your resume and see what High School and College you attended to make their decision. Consequently, not only must you go to a good High School but you must excel in it to reach your goals in life.

Below are a few options for different types of High Schools in Chicago that you might want to attend. However, if you do not live in Chicago, find a list of High Schools in your city that meets your requirements and select & record the one you like.

Type Of High Schools:
- Academic
- Private
- College
- Prep
- Military
- Trade
- Vocational

Additionally, when looking for a High School, one must consider their Rating and Ranking. How they stack up to one another could mean the difference of you attending a local Junior College or a highly sophisticated College. Also, how well you did in your Grammar School and Junior High School will determine whether or not you will be accepted into the High School of your choice.

Be mindful of the High School's Location because you do not want to attend a school that is located in a bad location. Here are some questions you and your parents need to go over:

- What do you have to do to get to school?
- Is it safe or dangerous?
- Is it near or far?
- What means of transportation do I need to get to school each day?
- Do I need to buy a Lunch or carry a Lunch?
- Are there certain Books Fees or other hidden Cost that I need to be concerned about?

Overall, looking for the right High School to attend will be an eye-opening experience for you and your parents. Listed below are some High Schools in Chicago that you can use to help make your decision. If you do not live in Chicago, go to the Internet and search for the High Schools in your city to make your determination of where you want to go to High School.

The High School Table

Here is **The High School Table** to give you an idea of what's available to you. After you have done your research Online, in the News Paper & Magazines, etc., record your selection on the Table. Fill in every category that applies. Your decision will have a lot to do with your future.

Below are a few options for different types of High Schools in Chicago that you might want to attend. However, if you do not live in Chicago, find a list of High Schools in your City, State, and/or Country that meets your requirements. Select & record the one you like.

- **195 High Schools In Chicago** - http://cps.edu/Schools/High_schools/Pages/HighschoolsIndex.aspx?Type=_1&Filter=CPSSchoolGrade=High%20school
- **List of CPS** - https://en.wikipedia.org/wiki/List_of_schools_in_Chicago_Public_Schools

Type	Rating/Ranking	Location	Transportation	Lunch	Books Fees	Cost
Vocational						
Academic						
Private						
College Prep						
Military						
Trade School						

College

There are a lot of things that go along with a selection of the right College. As you have already figured out by now, your Ambition and Career Goals are at stake. You may need your parents to help decide what school meets your needs and what you/they can afford.

College Education is the launching pad for your career choice. Therefore, you must have a good college education and sometimes, that depends on what college you attend. With that in mind, you must decide what direction you want to go in for your career. You must decide what are your career goals?

Now that you have an idea of what you want to be in life, you must search to find what college can I attend to reach my career goals? As with the High Schools, you might want to search out their Rating and Ranking among other colleges. Does the college of your choice offer Scholarships? What must you do to obtain a scholarship?

Please consider that everyone that applies for or is offered a scholarship; never reach their career goals because they have changed their focus from their career goals to whatever the scholarship is in. I say that because some may want to use the scholarship just to get into that college and think that they can go into whatever career goal they have set. Please make sure you read the fine print of that scholarship. If their requirements are that you pursue your education in the field of that scholarship, you will have to follow those requirements. You cannot vary away from them.

There are many different types of colleges. Below are some of the things that you must consider as you select the college of your choice.

- Do you want to attend a local Public/Community College or go away to a University?
- What Types of Colleges and Universities are in my area?
- What prerequisites do I need to attend that school?
- Where is that school located?
- What is the rating and ranking of that school?
- What is the Cost of:
  - Tuition
  - Cost
  - Books
  - Fees
  - Room & Board
- Should I choose a regular College or University? What's the difference?
- Should I attend a Private School or Public School?
- Should I go on to a Graduate School and get a Master's or Doctoral degree?
- Should I go into the Military?
- What Vocational colleges are there for me to choose from?

The college you attend can make the difference between what kind of job and career you get after you finish school. Therefore, prepare and choose wisely. Your life is at stake.

The College Table

Here is **The College Table**. After you have done your research Online, in the News Paper & Magazines, etc., record your selection on the Table. Fill in every category that applies. Your decision will have a lot to do with your future.

A List Of Colleges & Universities - http://www.studentadvisor.com/schools

Type	Prerequisites	Location	Rating/Ranking	Tuition	Cost
Public/Community					
University					
Private					
Graduate School					
Military					
Vocational					
Room & Board					
Books					
Total Cost					

BUDGETING & EXPENSES

What City Would You Like To Live In?

 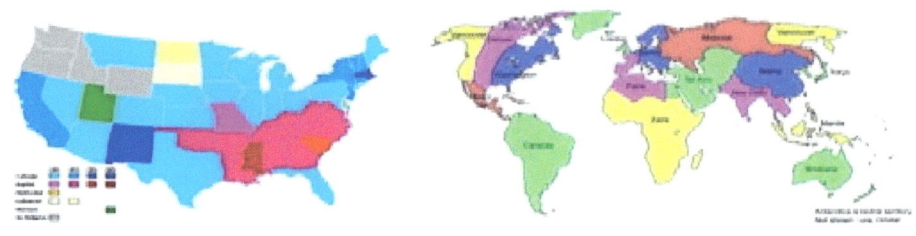

There are thousands of cities all over the world that are located in very beautiful places. The choices are overwhelming and the selections are phenomenal to look at. Some of these cities offer comforts that you never would expect and would love to have in your present location. If you investigate closely, you will find outstanding and gorgeous places to live.

However, the city where you would like to live, may not be your decision alone. Your job location or assignment may require you to travel or move. Additionally, your family may need to be with you and therefore require special needs within that city. For example, health may be a factor of your family that demands you to live in a certain location.

Go on the internet and see some of these cities and countries where you think you would like to live. Below are a few options for different types of cities in America that you can select from. Here are 50 Of The Best Cities To Live In America. http://247wallst.com/special-report/2014/09/17/americas-50-best-cities-to-live/12/

While you are looking these cities over, decide on the:
- Location
- Transportation

- Schools
- Stores
- Security
- Taxes
- Local Authorities
- State
- Country

Please consider the fact that, while a place may be beautiful to visit, can you afford to live there? How will you make your living in that beautiful city? Does this city fit within your Career Goals? Once you get married, does this city meet my family needs? It is your choice.

The City/Location Table

Here is **The City Where You Want To Live Table**. After you have done your research Online, in the News Paper & Magazines, record your selection on the Table. Fill in every category that applies. Your decision will have a lot to do with your future.

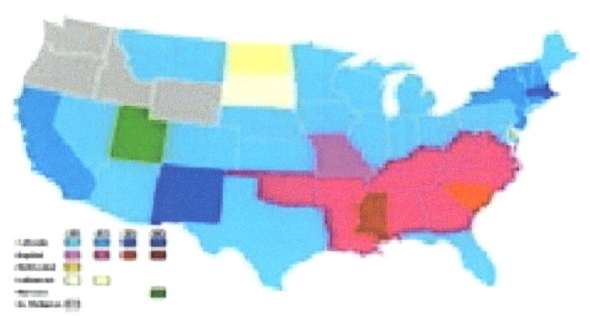

50 Of The Best Cities To Live In America - http://247wallst.com/special-report/2014/09/17/americas-50-best-cities-to-live/12/

Location	Transportation	Schools	Stores	Security	Taxes	Local Authorities
City						
State						
Country						

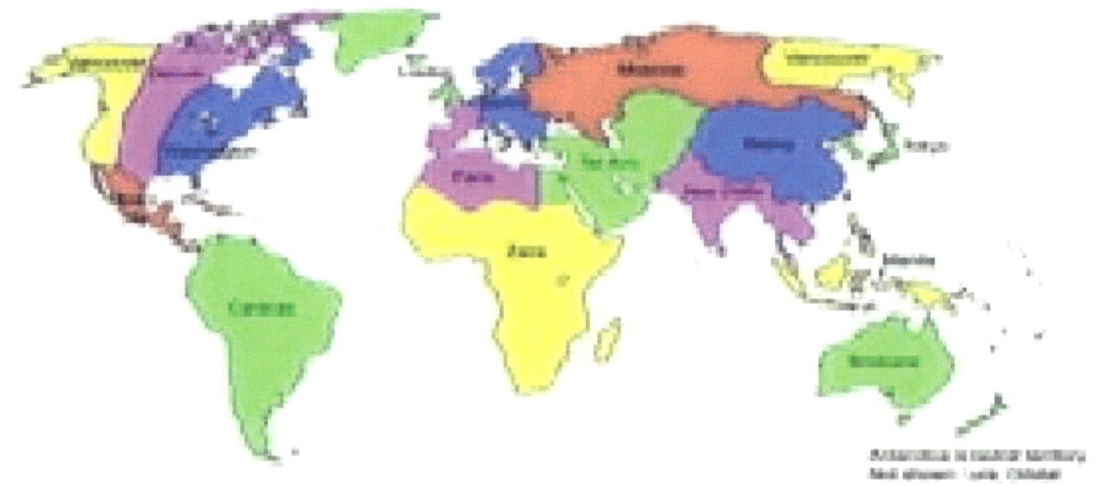

What Type Of Housing Do You Plan To Have?

There is so much involved in owning a home or renting an Apartment. Property Taxes play a great part of the decision of where to live for most people. Nevertheless, the Light Bill, Gas Bill, Telephone Bill, Water & Sewer Tax Bill and the Trash Removal Bill are some of the other responsibilities that you may have to assume too. Some of these Bills are included in the monthly Mortgage Payment or the Apartment Rent. Therefore, the type of housing or apartment you live in will have to be chosen wisely. With that said;

- Can you afford a house mortgage or is apartment rent better for you at this time?
- Are you moving in alone or do you have a family to care for now?
- Would a Condominium, a Co-Op or Townhouse be better for you at this time?
- Is the Location close enough to your job?
- How many Rooms do I need and how many does it offer?
- Is there safe Parking space for my vehicle?
- Will I have to be responsible for the Utilities?
- Are there any hidden Fees (janitorial, maid service, etc.) that I have to be responsible for?
- What type of Telephone do I want in my home, Landline or Cell Phone?

The Housing Table

Here is **The Type of Housing You Plan to Live Table**. After you have done your research Online, in the News Paper & Magazines, record your selection on the Table. Fill in every category that applies. Your decision will have a lot to do with you and your families' future.

(See Sunday's Classified Newspaper)

Type	Location	# Of Rooms	Parking	Utilities	Fees	Mortgage
Apartment						
House						
Condominium						
Co-Op						
Townhouse						
Light						
Gas						
Telephone						

The Type of Automobile/Vehicle You Want

This is a decision that is strictly your own to make. You will have to decide, according to your budget, the type of vehicle that you like or that you can afford. There are many different types to choose from. There are Cars (family and luxury), Trucks, SUV'S, Motorcycles, Three Wheel Cycles, Vans, Buses, etc. See your Newspaper or go online to review the different types of vehicles with all of their features. Consider their:

- Cost – What can you afford?
- Model – What do you like?
- Auto Club – Will you join an Auto Club?
- When looking for a vehicle:
  - Test Drive
  - Make sure it has a Spare Tire
  - Inspect the vehicle inside and out
  - If you can, make a trade in
  - What interest rate can you afford if you finance it?

As you select the vehicle of your choice, consider the maintenance cost and fuel cost every month. The appearance may look great, but can you afford to keep up its appearance from week to week? Consider how many miles per gallon will it do in the city and on the highway. Will you buy a brand new vehicle or a used one? Will you buy online or from a dealership? Will you finance the vehicle or will you pay cash?

The Automobile/Vehicle Table

Here is **The Type Of Automobile You Want To Drive Table**. After you have done your research Online, in the News Paper & Magazines, record your selection on the Table. Fill in every category that applies. Your decision will have a lot to do with you and your families' future. Decide according to your budget. Choose wisely and record your selection in the table below.

(See Sunday's Classified Newspaper)

Type	Model	Auto Club	Interest Rate %	Cost
Truck				
SUV				
Car				
Luxury				
Family				
Van				
Other				

Your Grocery Bill

Your Grocery Bill is going to depend on your Culture and City, Town or Country you were born in. What is acceptable in my country may not be very appetizing in yours. Nevertheless, we all have to eat to live. Consequently, we buy foods that are familiar with our area.

Some shop at the Grocery Store and others at the Market Place. Wherever you shop and whatever you eat, it's going to cost you. Some may choose to eat out at a local restaurant and others cook at home. In either case, you will have to set up your cost allowance to pay for your food.

For Your Information, a Staple Food is a food that makes up the dominant part of a population's diet. Staple Foods are eaten regularly and supply a major proportion of a person's energy, carbohydrates, proteins, fats and nutritional needs. Examples of Staple foods are fruits, potatoes, yams, grains, corn, seeds, cereals of wheat, barley, rye, or rice, root vegetables, milk, eggs, etc.

Some of these Staple Foods can be stored a long time without decay. What Staple Food you like and decide that they are good for you will be your choice. Look in the Newspaper and see what you like.

You might also want to consider Junk Food, every now and then. Chips, Candy, Pop, Juices, Hamburgers, Hot Dogs, might stir your fancy and you decide to go out and splurge a little bit at the local Junk Store Food for Dinner. That is going to be your choice. You will have to decide whether you are going to stick with family traditions, eat a healthy diet or let it all hang out and eat Junk Food. It is your body, your money, your life and your health. What you do with will be on you.

But know this; there are **Side Effects** of not eating right. According to a **FITDAY** article on the internet, entitled **Fast Food Nutrition: Junk Food's Effect On Your Body**, (http://www.fitday.com/fitness-articles/nutrition/healthy-eating/fast-food-nutrition-junk-foods-effect-on-your-body.html) Obesity, heart disease, diabetes, arthritis and may even a heart attack can be caused by Junk Foods.

All of these types of organ and body failures can be linked back to your diet. Some, if not all of them cannot be healed. You may have to live with these conditions until you die. Please be aware of your final outcome when you are older. What you eat now may cause Cancer when you are older, according to a **Better Health Channel** article entitled **Cancer and Food.** (https://www.betterhealth.vic.gov.au/health/conditionsandtreatments/cancer-and-food)

Seasoning is also a big hazard to your health. According to an article in **SFGATE** on the internet, entitled **What Are The Dangers Of Eating Salty Food?** (http://healthyeating.sfgate.com/dangers-eating-salty-foods-2439.html) High Blood Pressure, Kidney Stones, Cancer, Heart Attack & Strokes are all linked to foods having too much salt.

Hot peppers (Ghost Peppers) can also dangerous to the body and can cause seizures, heart attacks, and even death; according to an article in **Medical Daily**, entitled **Can Eating The World's Hottest Pepper Kill You? How Spicy Foods, Affect The Body**. (http://www.medicaldaily.com/can-eating-worlds-hottest-pepper-kill-you-how-spicy-foods-affect-body-330042) It would be to your advantage to investigate what spices are in the foods you select to eat. You may think that you can eat anything and walk away safe, but there are some foods, though tempting, that are not safe to eat, even for the toughest man or woman.

The Groceries Bill Table

Here is **The Groceries Bill Table**. After you have done your research on the News Paper for the latest sales, record your selection on the Table. Fill in every category that applies. Your decision will have a lot to do with you and your families' future. Decide according to your budget. Choose wisely and record your selection in the table below.

(See your Newspaper for food items on sale)

Type	Staples	Fruit/Meats/Vegetables	Seasoning	Shopping Day	Cost

Your Clothing Allowance

Ever since the beginning of time, men have been dressing in clothing that met the times and season of that era. Today, there are all types of new clothing fashions and styles that are coming out, as we speak. New trends fill the Fashion World all around the Globe.

They are very beautiful and expensive. But what fashion and style fit you? Just like every man cannot be in the Circus, climb Mt. Everest, or go to the moon, every fashion style does not fit you. You are a different person than everyone else. Your taste of clothing is as different from your friends, as the east is from the west.

Even though you know that all styles don't fit everybody, nor look good on everybody, you buy it anyway. You are trying to avoid being ridiculed (dished, talked about) by your so-called friends. You are trying to fit in with your friends and wear the latest pants styles, shirts, gym shoes, coats and hairstyle that come out. You will have to stop that way of thinking and become your own person and not be dictated to by your friends.

It is sad to say, but some clothing might be dangerous to wear in certain neighborhoods because the different Gangs have adopted certain clothing as part of their identity. If you wear those clothes in that neighborhood and you are not part of that gang, they will take offense and hurt you or even kill you.

Another situation to consider, there may be that someone wants to wear that style of clothing so bad that they will steal it from you because they don't have the money to buy it for themselves. Consequently, you must be cautious when selecting clothing today.

However, when you are planning for your future, you must **Dress To Impress**. I say that because your first impression you give to people on the job you apply for will be the lasting impression they will remember. Sometimes, the mere fact that you dress in business attire when you applied for that job, will be the possible cause of you landing that job.

Now the question is, will you dress to be fashionable or for your job? Will you dress to please your friends or wear the style that you like, regardless of what your friends think? Remember, you are the one buying your clothes and not your friends. Your job may require you to dress a certain way that your friends might not understand or agree with. But you are your own man/woman now. Don't let your friends dictate to you how to dress. It is your decision about what you wear and what you can afford.

You have got to think for yourself. You are spending your money, from your job to support yourself and/or your family. You must decide on where you can afford to shop. You must decide on what winter or summer outfits to buy. Not only that, but you must now buy your own underwear and footwear at whatever quality and cost you can afford.

The Clothing Allowance Table

Here is *The Clothing Allowance Table*. After you have done your research Online, in the News Paper & Magazines, record your selection on the Table. Fill in every category that applies. Your decision will have a lot to do with you and your families' future. Decide according to your taste and your budget. Choose wisely and record your selection in the table below.

(See Sunday's Newspaper Sales)

Types	Shopping Location	Winter	Summer	Cost
Underwear				
Outerwear				
Footwear				
Quality				

Furniture

Like clothing is a matter of personal taste, so also is Furniture. The Furniture your parents purchased when you were young may not be what you like for your home or apartment today. Times have changed and so did the fashion and styles of furniture. How you dress your house or apartment will be strictly up to your taste. Therefore, you will have to search the Newspapers, Magazines or Online ads of furniture stores and styles to find what you like.

With that thought in mind, go back to the section that deals with what selection you made for your house or apartment. Look for the type of house or apartment's décor. Decide on what type of furniture that will go well with the type of house or apartment you have selected.

Do you want narrow type furniture for this apartment, because you are not planning on staying there long? Do you want that furniture that the movers have a hard time getting it through the front door? You may think that that chair or couch may look good in your living room. But does it fit your lifestyle? Does it give you the appearance that you like? There are many types and styles of furniture out there, from all over the world.

If you are married, you and your spouse must agree on your home's furnishings. You might want your own Man-Cave or Woman's Closet, but does your partner agree with it? Will it bring you closer together or drive you further apart? If children are involved, then you must shop to accommodate your children as well. Sometimes the husband has to step back and allow the wife to choose the furniture because she has a better eye for it than some men.

Quality and cost are going to help you make your decision. Depending on your financing, you may have to get a less quality bit of furniture until you can save for a higher quality one. Or you may be able to purchase that high-quality piece of furniture and don't look back. It is all up to your taste and what you can afford.

You will have to plan and organize your purchases of furniture around your lifestyle. You may not want a fully furnished Dining Room. You might be comfortable eating at the Kitchen table. You may not want to completely furnish the Living Room because you need to buy your Bed Room furniture first.

The Old English or The French Provincial type of furnishing might not be your style, especially with all of the latest modern technology that has come out. You may very content with a Modern Looking Bathroom and Kitchen. To you, it might be easier to keep clean and give you that unique appearance that you like. There are so many varieties of types and styles to choose from. You will have to do your research and find what you like.

The Furniture Table

Here is The Furniture Table. After you have done your research Online, in the News Paper & Magazines, record your selection on the Table. Fill in every category that applies. Your decision will have a lot to do with you and your families' future. Decide according to your budget. Choose wisely and record your selection in the table below.

(See Sunday's Newspaper Sales or Online Furniture Stores)

Type/Style	TV	Living Room	Dining Room	Kitchen	Bed Room	Cost
French Provincial						
Modern						
Old English						
Modern						

Insurances

An arrangement by which a company gives customers financial protection against loss or harm such as theft or illness in return for payment premium is called Insurance. Believe it or not, everyone will need some type of Insurance someday, or sometime in their lifetime. As you age, your body breaks down and needs to be repaired. The Insurance premium pays the cost of those physical repairs; doctor visits, hospital stays, and surgeries.

Consequently, you need to select a company that will give you coverage for the Insurance that you need. Here are some of the types of Insurance you are going to need:

- Life Insurance (Family Plan if you are married)
- Health Insurance (Family Plan if you are married)
- Dental Insurance (Family Plan if you are married)
- Eye Care Insurance (Family Plan if you are married)
- Plan for Retirement, such as a 401K plan
- House Insurance
- Automobile Insurance

Additionally, some companies will give you Stock Options as part of your benefits package. Having these benefits will assure you and your family's safety and security throughout your career. If your job pays for these insurances, do not be overly concerned about the salary. The costs of these Insurances are far better for you than a large salary because the job is paying your Insurance for you. It is not coming out of your take-home pay.

The Insurance Table

Here is **The Insurance Table**. After you have done your research Online, in the News Paper & Magazines, record your selection on the Table. Fill in every category that applies. Your decision will have a lot to do with you and your families' future. Decide according to your budget.

Consequently, you need to select a company that will give you coverage for the insurance that you need. Below are just some of the Insurance Companies that may meet your requirements. Once you have found one you like, record it in the table below.

Top 10 Insurance companies in the US - http://www.thetruthaboutinsurance.com/top-ten-insurance-companies-in-the-united-states/

Type	Location	Cost
Life		
Health		
Dental		
Eye Glass		
House		
Automobile		

Banking

A Bank is a business where people deposit, withdraw, borrow and store their money. It is an establishment for loans, exchange or issuance of money, for the extension of credit and for facilitating the transmission of funds. Banking has been around for as far back as 2000 BC In Assyria and Babylonia, according to Wikipedia. So, as you can see, it is nothing new.

There are all types of Banks in the world. The one you choose will have to be one that is close to you for your immediate banking needs. You may select them to handle your Mortgage, Car Loan, Safety Deposit Box and your Savings and Checking accounts. You should also see if they offer Credit Cards, Certificate Deposit, Savings Bonds and Identity Theft Security. It is very important that you find a bank that you can trust. With today's technological explosion, there are all types of Scams in the world today. Make sure you are comfortable with the bank's policies and security.

This is your money and you must find a bank that you are confident with handling it. Therefore, you might have to investigate a bank first, to see if they are listed in The Better Business Bureau (BBB), as a safe choice to do business with. The BBB collects and provides free business reviews on more than 4 million businesses. (Wikipedia - https://en.wikipedia.org/wiki/Better_Business_Bureau) Most of the time, if a bank is listed with the BBB, then they are a bank that can be trusted. If you have any complaint with a company that is listed with the BBB, they will help to solve your complaint.

That is why it is so important that you do your research first before you put your money in any institution call a bank. If you are married, that bank will be a good place to save and store your money for a troublesome rainy day or plans to expand your family.

The Banking Table

Here is **The Banking Table**. After you have done your research Online, in the News Paper & Magazines, record your selection on the Table. Fill in every category that applies. Your decision will have a lot to do with you and your families' future. Check the list below of banks on the Website and see if any of them meets your requirements, then fill in the table below.

Top 10 Banks in the US - http://money.usnews.com/money/blogs/my-money/2015/02/12/the-10-best-banks-of-2015

Name Of Bank	Type	$ To Save
	Checking	
	Saving	
	Stocks	
	Bonds	
	Mutual Funds	

TOTAL LIVING EXPENSES

Now that you have arrived at the end of your cost estimates, and filled in all of the Tables at the end of each section, we need to collect all of that information to see what your **Total Living Expenses** are going to be. Once you find that out, then you will know what The Total Income you are going to need to sustain the lifestyle that you want to live. Therefore, go back to each section and take the Total Cost of that section and list it here for your **Total Cost Of Living Analysis**.

Total Living Expenses Table

#	Items	Cost
1.	High School	
2.	College	
3.	City/Location	
4.	Housing	
5.	Automobile	
6.	Groceries	
7.	Clothing	
8.	Furniture	
9.	Insurance	
10.	Banking	
Total Cost Of Living		

Total Income Needed For Your Lifestyle Table

    With the sum of your total cost of living, look and see if this is the salary you will need to make to maintain your lifestyle each year. Decide what is the Highest salary you need to make and what is the lowest you need for your life and or family.

    This salary total is a general indicator of what you must do now, for the lifestyle you plan for your future. This salary total shows how much money you must make to support yourself and your family.

Salary	**Amount**
Highest	$
Lowest	$

SEX, ALCOHOL & DRUGS

If there is anything that can derail you off your path and kill the flame of your desire to change your future, it is Premarital Sex/Fornication, Alcohol, and Drugs. These three things deal with the feelings of a person. Being young, you always want to feel good. However, if you don't know it, let me tell you, good feelings don't last very long! The good feeling one gets the first time it will drive a person to do it over and over and over again, trying to reach that first plateau they experienced.

But there is an old saying that says; **"Everything That Feels Good To Ya, Is Not Good For Ya."** Wherefore, it might feel good to you but what are the consequences that go along with it? Having Premarital Sex/Fornication, drinking Alcohol and doing Drugs affect your body in ways that directly changes your life and your future. These three things can take you places you that never wanted to be and now, you do not want to leave or cannot leave.

Wanting to be like your friends or searching for good feelings is like getting on a train that is unstoppable. DO NOT GET ON THAT TRAIN BECAUSE, ONCE YOU ARE ON IT, YOU CANNOT STOP IT NOR GET OFF IT ON YOUR OWN! IT WILL RUIN THE FUTURE THAT YOU PLANED TO HAVE AND STOP YOU FROM REACHING YOUR GOALS IN LIFE!

Parents, it is up to you to educate your child about these dangerous issues. You are obligated for getting them to a place of independence and self-reliance. Up until that time, he or she is your responsibility. Your guidance at this point in their lives is critical to their proper development. Wherefore, realizing the weight of the choices your child has to make, refer to your personal experiences and tell them what your mistakes were and what they should do to avoid them.

As a Minister, I used The Word Of God (The King James Authorized Version Of The Bible) as a guide to point out to my children what God says about Fornication and Alcohol. I pointed out to them that fornication is a sin against their own bodies (I Corinthians 6:18, Ephesians 5:3) and that getting married was the way to avoid it. (I Corinthians 7:2). I showed them what The Word Of God says about alcohol in Proverbs 20:1, Ephesians 5:18, how that God does not want us to drink and how that these sins will keep them out of The Kingdom Of God. (Galatians 5:21, I Corinthians 6:9-10)

As a father, I testified to my children about my fornication and drinking of alcohol. I told them of the disease that I caught while fornicating. I warned them against drinking alcohol and how I suffered in my body from the LATENT EFFECTS of it. These interventions acted as a deterrent for them when it came to drugs. Since alcohol had almost killed their father, they wanted nothing to do with drugs.

Final Words

Now that you have come to the end of this program, what are your thoughts? Do you think you will make the salary you need to sustain the lifestyle you want with the grades you are making in school right now? If so, then **GREAT JOB! YOU ARE ON TARGET! KEEP UP THE GOOD WORK!** But if not, then you have got to buckle down and make the right choices, to make the right grades, to make the salary, to live the life you want. Review your plans for your future.

Was the Ambition you selected the best one for the lifestyle you want to live? Was the Career you chose connected to your Ambition? Will you find an Occupation that will pay you a salary that will meet your needs? What do you think about it now? Are you happy with your results? What are you going to do with your results?

What are you really interested in; being Successful, rich, wealthy or in good health and free from debt. What's more important to you? There are those who are rich but confined to a wheelchair, being a paraplegic or quadriplegic. Others are billionaires, but look down on their fellow man. Lastly, there are those that don't make much, but they are happy and content with themselves and family.

It is time for you to make a very important decision for your future. You will have to live with your decision and not your parents. You will not be able to blame anyone if you don't succeed and reach your Career Goals. So, *What Do You Want To Be When You Grow Up?*

WHAT AM I GOING TO DO FOR THE REST OF MY LIFE?

WHAT AM I GOING TO DO WITH MY LIFE?

WHAT DO I WANT TO BE WHEN I GROW UP?

References:

Graphics & Art Work are from Microsoft Office Professional Plus 2010 DVD

The Internet:

- Options- Over 12, 000 Careers - http://www.careerplanner.com/ListOfCareers.cfm

- Salaries & Jobs - http://www.salarylist.com/jobs/Other-Salary.htm

- 100 Of The Best Jobs - http://money.usnews.com/careers/best-jobs/rankings/the-100-best-jobs

- 195 High Schools In The Chicagoland Area - http://cps.edu/Schools/High_schools/Pages/HighschoolsIndex.aspx?Type=1&Filter=CPSSchoolGrade=High%20school

- List of CPS - https://en.wikipedia.org/wiki/List_of_schools_in_Chicago_Public_Schools

- A List Of Colleges & Universities – http://www.studentadvisor.com/schools

- 50 Of The Best Cities To Live In America - http://247wallst.com/special-report/2014/09/17/americas-50-best-cities-to-live/12/

- Top 10 Insurance companies in the US - http://www.thetruthaboutinsurance.com/top-ten-insurance-companies-in-the-united-states/

- Top 10 Banks In The US - http://money.usnews.com/money/blogs/my-money/2015/02/12/the-10-best-banks-of-2015

- Famous People With College Degrees

  http://www.huffingtonpost.com/gobankingrates/20-rich-and-famous-commun_b_7546150.html

  https://mic.com/articles/86351/19-celebrities-who-graduated-from-really-good-colleges#.W8zU9VotF

  https://blackamericaweb.com/playlist/rap-stars-with-a-college-degree/item/70709

- The King James Authorized Version Of The Bible